chairseven books

THE
BEST
LITTLE
MARKETING
PLAN

A simple workbook for building a great marketing strategy.

SEAN HARRY

Published in the United States of America by Chairseven
Creative, LLC, Portland, Oregon.

ISBN 978-0-9961020-0-1

1. THE MARKETING PLAN
The core elements of a marketing plan include:

2. THE MARKETING CAMPAIGN
Activate your marketing plan with these five steps:

1

The Marketing Plan

Everyone tells you that you need a marketing plan in order to grow your small business. But what exactly is a marketing plan? How do you create one? How do you use it?

Introduction

This book will take a look at the core elements of a marketing plan and help you discover how to put them to use through a specific marketing campaign.

The Internet is full of people who promise to teach you how to market and sell millions of units. They claim to have "the solution" for all of your marketing problems. Many small businesses take a haphazard approach to marketing, which often costs too much and is usually ineffective. A strategic marketing plan will help keep you on a path toward reaching your goals and growing your business.

Without a plan it's easy to be tossed by the winds of every marketing opportunity that comes down the pike, and without campaigns you have no way to implement your plan. This book will guide you through building an outline of your marketing activities for a year. The outline is intended to help you achieve strategic business goals by developing a cohesive marketing effort which can then be implemented as campaigns.

The activities in this book will walk you through the specific steps for developing each of the elements of an overall marketing strategic plan. Once you have completed the worksheets for each section, you can transfer the information to the templates at the end of the book, and presto, you'll be ready to share and implement the marketing plan for your business!

MARKETING IS NOT SELLING

Before we get started on your Marketing Plan there's something you need to know: marketing is not selling. Sales and marketing are related, but they are different. Selling is the act of "sealing the deal" or "creating a customer." Marketing, on the other hand, is simply about creating awareness and keeping a potential customer's attention until they are ready to buy.

My favorite professor in grad school defined marketing as "renting out space in the mind of the consumer." When you engage in marketing activities, you want to grab the attention of a potential buyer and plant a seed in their brain. Your marketing is intended to help your potential customer think of you when they need your product or service. Other than their attention, the point of marketing requires very little from the potential buyer.

The responsibility of marketing lies with the marketer. That's why it's best to tie marketing to an emotional space, a mind space, or a feeling space.

To do this, ask yourself "What does my customer want or need?" and "How can my product (or service) fulfill that need?" When you can explain a product in terms that your customer is looking for, you are marketing successfully and effectively.

There is a commercial that I see on a regular basis that always grabs my attention. The product is something we sometimes think of as kid's cereal, but the marketing message is directed at me—a middle aged man with a propensity for high blood pressure. The product is Cheerios®, something that I have eaten all my life. When my children were small we gave them Cheerios as a way to keep them busy or to help them learn to feed themselves. As an adult, I am learning that the cereal has another, more powerful application—reducing cholesterol.

To get their message across, the good folks at Cheerios show a lovely interaction between a grandpa and his grandson. Grandpa and grandson are both "studying for a test" while eating breakfast. The child, naturally, wants to score high on his math test. The grandfather, however, wants to score low on his cholesterol test—something Cheerios can help him with.

Now, the advertisers don't expect me to buy the product when I see this commercial. They don't expect me to get up and go to the store to purchase a box right then and there. I know this because they run the commercial at about 8 o'clock in the evening when I am securely fastened to my easy chair. They know me well enough to entice me with a grandpa/grandchild relationship, but they also know me well enough to expect that nothing short of a natural disaster, or a comfy bed, will get me out of the recliner!

Selling and marketing are not the same thing. These ads are not intended to sell me anything. They are simply trying to plant a seed in my brain that sets off an alarm the next time I am on the cereal aisle at the grocery store.

They know I'll be pushing the cart thinking, "Hey, these fruit-y things look great!" But the little alarm in my head will say, "Remember? Cheerios are good for your cholesterol. They will help you grow older and stick around longer to play with your grandchildren!" So I reach out and grab the O's.

Marketing is renting out space in the mind of the consumer. That's why jingles are so effective. Jingles can reside in your mind and help you remember the product. (What WOULD you do for a Klondike® bar?)!

MARKETING IS RENTING OUT SPACE IN THE MIND OF THE CONSUMER.

Define & Analyze Your Market

The first essential marketing element is the ability to clearly identify your target market. By clearly identifying your market you will be able to create a marketing campaign that cuts through the noise and plants a seed in the mind of your consumers. Clear identification of the people you are targeting allows you to create a message that is tailor-made for your customers. They will be able to hear you through the cacophony of messages with which they are bombarded every day. When you clearly define your customer and their needs, you are creating a target for your marketing activities and thereby taking the first step in "renting out space" in the mind of your customer.

Consider this, according to studies, each day you are inundated with an average of 5,000 marketing messages. So is your customer. What can you do to cut through that clutter to help them find you? A general, broad, "everybody come" message isn't going to do it. In order to get your customer's attention you have to grab them by the lapel and say, "This is important for you. Please pay attention."

Below are the key pieces you need to identify in order to create a clear market description and analysis.

SIZE OF YOUR MARKET

How big is your potential market? This is the most basic of marketing questions, because it helps determine if there is a viable market for your products or services. The goal is to narrow your market to a niche that is large enough for you to grab a reasonable percentage of, but not be too broad. If the size of your market is too small, you will have trouble reaching them, and if the description of your market is too broad, you will not be able to attract customers. The key is to focus your market enough to have a clear picture of who you are targeting while simultaneously having a large enough pool from which to draw.

GEOGRAPHIC DESCRIPTION

Your geographic description will help you know where to apply your marketing efforts for maximum results. Where is your target market located? Are you going to meet with these people face to face? Are you going to them, or are they coming to you? Will you reach them remotely? What methods will you use to reach them (website, social media, direct mail)?

DEMOGRAPHIC DESCRIPTION

Demographics are statistics that describe details of your target market. Think of demographics as things you can count. They are the statistical facts about your target market.

If you sell directly to consumers (i.e. "Business to Consumers") you will define demographics according to: age, gender, marital status, annual income, family size and make-up, height, weight, length of hair . . . basically everything you can describe about the person that is important to understanding their needs.

If your customers are other businesses (i.e. "Business to Business") you will describe their demographics in terms of how big the company is, how long they have been in business, how many employees they have, their business structure, key players, etc.

PSYCHOGRAPHIC DESCRIPTION

Psychographic indicators help you understand what makes your customers tick. Psychographics are the key values and motivators of your customers. Knowing what "moves" your customers helps you get inside their head to know what they need and how they need it. Whenever possible you want to match your core values up with the core values of your customers. This makes it easy for them to remember and buy from you.

BEHAVIORAL CHARACTERISTICS

Behavior characteristics will help you find customers according to the things they are already doing. What are the behavior patterns of your customers that relate to your product or service? Where do they go? What sports do they participate in? How do they communicate with their friends and family? Where do they hang out? What similar products do they purchase?

When you know the behavior patterns of your customers you can show up where they are most likely to show up. Your marketing will speak directly to them if you know what they do.

Describing your target market is the first step in developing a successful marketing plan. Having a clear definition and analysis of your clients is an important step in knowing how to reach them with your message. Without it you are doomed to be just another bit of noise in an overly noisy world.

SWOT Analysis

SWOT stands for "Strengths, Weaknesses, Opportunities and Threats" and it's one of the best ways to conduct a competitive market analysis for your product or service. This popular tool will help you focus on your internal capabilities and align them with external opportunities. When done correctly a SWOT Analysis will help you find a distinct advantage over your competitors. It will guide your marketing efforts for maximum impact.

Here's how the SWOT Analysis works:

INTERNAL STRENGTHS

By defining your internal strengths you will gain a clear understanding of what your capabilities are. Internal strengths may come from resources or processes you own. They may be a "special sauce" or "secret formula." Your strengths may include specialized skills or knowledge of your personnel. Whatever your strengths, clearly identifying them will help you utilize them to your advantage.

Here are some questions to ask when conducting an internal strengths assessment:

- What is your unique value to your customers?
- What do you do best?
- What do you want to be known for?
- What are the best qualities of your products or services?
- What is your business so good at that you could do it with your eyes closed and one hand tied behind your back?

INTERNAL WEAKNESSES

Many small businesses spend a great deal of time and money trying to improve their weaknesses. I recommend you take the opposite approach. When you focus on your strengths and mitigate your weaknesses you maximize your potential for success. It's much easier to improve on a strength, rather than a weakness, and it will often provide more bang for your buck.

Use these questions to help you assess your weaknesses:
- What don't you do well?
- What capabilities are you lacking? Do you need them, or is it better to pay somebody else to do them?
- What would you rather let your competitors and/or key partners focus on?

EXTERNAL OPPORTUNITIES

Government regulations, new inventions, political changes and shifting social norms can have a strong effect on opportunities and threats to your business. These external factors are things that you have no control over. You can't create or change them. You can, however, leverage them strategically to grow your business.

These are good questions to ask when conducting an external scan:
- What is happening in your target market that makes room for the success of your products or services?
- What opportunities are on the horizon that you could tap into?
- Are there any new laws or regulations taking effect that you could leverage?
- What are the trends in your segment?
- What's going out of style with your customers?
- What's coming into style?

EXTERNAL THREATS

Just as economic, social, or political activities can provide opportunities to your business, they can also present a threat. Things that are happening outside your doors can make a product or service unnecessary, boring, or even obsolete. You do not have control over the way your customers wear their hair, or the color of car they prefer, or even political regulations. Being aware of these external threats will help you steer clear of them in your marketing activities.

Try answering these questions to come up with a list of external threats:

- What might prohibit or restrict your ability to reach your target market?
- What trends are impacting your industry in a negative way?
- What external change might happen that could severely cripple your business?

You will use the findings of your SWOT analysis to leverage your internal strengths and match them up with external opportunities. At the same time your goal is to mitigate internal weaknesses and avoid external threats as much as possible. The SWOT Analysis will give you a clearer picture of what to do (or not to do) as you plan your marketing actions.

Figure 1.1 demonstrates what a SWOT Analysis might look like for a professional speaker/trainer who is focusing on services to banks, finance professionals, and insurance agencies. It is accompanied by a blank worksheet for you to conduct your own SWOT analysis.

Figure 1.1 - SWOT Analysis Example

Strengths

- Effective at helping individuals and companies delineate their Unique Value Proposition (i.e. "Personal Brand").
- Extensive experience training and speaking on the topic.
- Well-known and highly respected for speaking and training abilities.
- Provides great value – clients are ENGAGED and happy with what they receive and willingly refer him to colleagues.
- High quality promotional materials.
- eBook available through Amazon.

Weaknesses

- Lack of specific experience in the banking, finance and insurance industries.
- Doesn't yet have a published book on the topic other than the eBook (but working on it).
- Doesn't have a large budget to purchase advertising or develop "slick" marketing collateral.

Opportunities

- Distrust in the general public of bankers, financial professionals and insurance agents.
- Recent studies on the value of trust — "Companies with high trust levels generated total returns to shareholders at 3X that of companies with low levels or trust."
- Companies are positioned for growth after recent recession.
- Need for new tools — old ones are either stale, outdated, or simply don't work in this environment.

Threats

- Companies may have more pressing needs and not feel an urgent need to develop "trusting relationships."
- Target companies prefer to provide in-house training.
- Target companies may have limited budgets for training, option to focus on offerings that provide CEU credits for certification of licensing requirements.

Complete your own SWOT analysis here:

Strengths

Weaknesses

Opportunities

Threats

Value Proposition and Positioning Statement

Now that you have conducted a thorough assessment of your target market, and have looked closely at your strengths, weaknesses, opportunities and threats with a SWOT Analysis, it's time to develop your Unique Value Proposition (UVP) and your Positioning Statement. The UVP and Positioning Statement help you describe exactly how your product or service brings something of worth to your customers and why they should choose you rather than ignore you.

UNIQUE VALUE PROPOSITION

Your Unique Value Proposition is your brand or the promise of what you will provide to your customers. It helps your customers answer the question, "Why should I buy from you rather than your competition?" Until you know that, you will have a hard time reaching your customers. If you don't know why they should buy from you, it's a safe bet they don't know either.

The UVP should be formulated from the customer's point of view so they can see that what you are offering is what they are looking for. A UVP is not so much a statement of WHAT you do, rather it is a statement of what your customers GET from what you do. There can be a big difference.

Let's say your product is a child's bike seat. You have a product that makes it easier for your customer to transport children on their bike. It's a child carrier that fastens to a bike. Relatively simple. Relatively straight forward.

However, the customer receives much more than that. They get the satisfaction of spending time with their child. They get a product that lets them know their child is safe while on the back of their bike. They receive a tool for bonding with their child as they ride through the countryside together. That's a whole lot more than just "a child carrier that fastens to your bike!"

When you state your Unique Value Proposition you must try to do so from your customer's point of view. Ask yourself, "If I were buying this product, what would be most important to me?" Stand in their shoes and ask yourself what they feel, see, hear, say and do. Use their words to describe how your product or service will improve their life.

The following questions will help you get started in creating your unique positioning:

- What do your competitors do that your customers don't like? Does your UVP tell how you do it better?
- What characteristics or personality traits can you put into your value proposition? How do those appeal to your customers?
- What kinds of images or metaphorical devices speak to your customers? Can you use those in your UVP?
- Are you driven by a particular mission or desire to change the world? Does that show up in your value proposition?
- What is the end goal of your customers? What to they REALLY want that would drive them to your product or service?
- What are the alternatives for your customers to choosing your product or service? Would they choose your competitors? Would they choose not to purchase? Why?

Flowers vs. Romance

Which is more effective: selling flowers or selling romance? There is a big difference! If you sell flowers you are selling a commodity that people can get for free. Flowers pretty much grow all by themselves in a garden or even a crack in the sidewalk. You can buy flowers cheap at any grocery store.

Romance, on the other hand, is a bit more challenging to provide. Romance is an experience, a relationship, a memory. Which would you rather buy, a commodity (flowers) or a relationship (romance)?

It may have taken a lot of time to grow the flower, to get the color just right, or to ship the flower. Things like the length of the stem and cutting the flower at just the right time make a difference in how long the flowers will last. You may want to show your customers how smart you are about flowers, but honestly, nobody cares!

If you want to sell more flowers, I recommend you focus on why people buy flowers. Flowers make your house smell nice. Flowers brighten up the room. Flowers will help you romance your lover. If you are in the dog house, flowers will help smooth things over.

These are the BENEFITS of flowers. Benefits are what the flowers do for you. Details about the flowers (color, stem length, etc) are the FEATURES of the flowers. Florists who focus on the benefits of flowers to their customers sell more flowers, hands down. Very few people want flowers, but everybody wants a little romance!

Many businesses make the mistake of "selling flowers." In their marketing activities they talk about the features of their products or services. Too many websites and brochures concentrate on specifications of the product. They zero in on the color or the cool features of a product. They are just selling flowers. What do you think would happen if these businesses focused their marketing on the benefits of their product to the customer? Instead of emphasizing what the product is made of, what might happen if they gave a snapshot of how the product will make the customer's life better?

What about you? Are you focusing on the features of your product? Or are you focusing on the benefits your customers get from your product? Are you selling flowers, or are you selling romance? Focus on the benefits to your customer and you will sell more. Hands down. ▪

| Your Unique Value Proposition is: |

_____

_____

_____

_____

_____

_____

_____

_____

POSITIONING STATEMENT

Your Positioning Statement is similar to your Unique Value Proposition in that it also helps define your position in the marketplace. The difference between the two is that the Positioning Statement explains where your product or service fits in relation to other products and services out there. A positioning statement lets you know where you are in comparison to similar options.

Positioning statements are typically "in-house" items, and for a good reason. Would you want your competitors to know the specific niche you intend to carve out for yourself? No way!

In 2010 Steve Jobs gave us a good example of how one company (Apple®) intended to position a new product (one of my favorite devices, the iPad®) as it was being introduced to the world. An article from The New York Times® in January 2010 hinted at the positioning statement of the iPad with the headline, "With Its Tablet, Apple Blurs Line Between Devices". The article quoted Steve Jobs as he introduced the iPad to the world:

The iPad "is so much more intimate than a laptop, and it's so much more capable than a smartphone with its gorgeous screen," he said in presenting the device to a crowd of journalists and Apple employees... "It's phenomenal to hold the Internet in your hands."

– The New York Times, January 27, 2010

It is obvious that Jobs (and Apple) meant for the iPad to occupy a position right between the iPhone® (or smart phone) and the laptop.

Clear articulation of your Unique Value Proposition and Positioning Statements help you provide a clear description of the value you bring to customers. These two elements are powerful parts of your Marketing Plan.

The position you intend to occupy in the market is:

_____

_____

_____

_____

_____

_____

_____

Annual Goals, Quarterly Objectives and Budget

By now you should have a clear description of your target market. You know who your competitors are, and you understand how to combine your internal strengths with external opportunities to clearly articulate both your Unique Value Proposition and your Market Position.

In order to effectively promote a specific product or service you must develop a specific marketing campaign. Now it's time to answer two important marketing questions. The answer to these questions will help you create successful marketing campaigns.

Question 1. What goals do you have for your marketing efforts this year (or quarter)?

Question 2. How much will you budget in order to achieve those goals?

These two questions are critical for your ability to plan and succeed in your marketing ventures. They lay out the scope of your marketing campaign and help you put together a plan to achieve it. Use the space on the next page to answer them for yourself.

What are your annual marketing goals?

1. _____

2. _____

3. _____

4. _____

5. _____

How much is your marketing budget for the year?

$ _____

SETTING SMART GOALS

SMART goals are: Specific, Measurable, Achievable, Realistic and Time-Oriented goals . Marketing can be expensive in terms of both time and money, so setting quantifiable goals that will allow you to measure your marketing initiatives will help you know whether or not they are working. Setting SMART goals allows for you to measure success and calculate a return on your investment (ROI). There is a time honored saying in business, "If you can measure it, you can improve it."

I recommend setting three to four SMART goals for the entire year. Too many goals means you are not focused enough. Too few and your success will be limited.

Once you have set your annual goals, you will be able to break those down into quarterly objectives. These quarterly objectives will become your marketing campaigns. Campaigns can range from 2 weeks to 2 months, depending on what you are trying to accomplish. Campaigns have a very clear target in mind, they make you money! String a few successful marketing campaigns together and you will have a successful year!

Begin your campaign plan by clearly defining specific and realistic objectives. Use the SMART approach here to focus your objectives.

Once your campaign objectives are set, it's time to complete a budget. If you have run similar campaigns in the past then you have some hard numbers to plug into your budget. If not, you will have to make a strategic guess and create a pro forma budget. If you plan to work with graphic designers or have a sales force, your budget is necessary to help them determine the scope of work they can do for you. Here are some things that you want to include in your budget:

• Revenue Targets—How much money do you expect each campaign to bring in? This is one of the easiest ways to assess whether or not a campaign has been successful.

• New customers or subscribers—How many new customers or subscribers has your marketing campaign attracted?

• Packaging, warehousing and shipping costs—What are the costs associated with handling your materials?

• Campaign production and delivery costs—How much is it going to cost to create and distribute your brochures and other marketing materials? Be sure to adequately account for time associated with email marketing and other "free" campaign tools such as Twitter, Facebook and Pinterest. The tools may be free, but there is still a cost to you for using them—your time.

- Margins—After your costs have been deducted, how much is left over? This is the margin, or "gross revenue." You want to make sure your margins are large enough to justify your marketing efforts. If not, back to the drawing board.

- Time—How much time will you and your staff spend on each campaign? What benchmarks do you need to hit in order to accomplish your goals on time? Is there a "point of no return" built into your campaigns—a specific date where you stop the campaign if things aren't working out the way you planned? Sometimes it's better to pull the plug rather than spend good money on something you know early on isn't going to work.

- Reviewing and analyzing the success of your campaigns (including both time and money) —It's a best practice in business to schedule a time to review lessons learned so you can keep the good and dump the bad next time.

Setting clear quarterly objectives and establishing a workable budget will ensure success in your marketing efforts. Remember, "plan your work, then work your plan."

The Marketing Campaign

The marketing campaign is where the rubber meets the road—or rather, where your market analysis, external opportunities and your own competencies meet your target market. Simply put, campaigns are what make you money.

The Marketing Mix

So far you have clearly defined your marketing goals and objectives. You have also established a budget of the time and money you plan to spend on marketing. These activities outline the big picture of where your marketing is headed in the coming year. Now it's time to focus on a specific action plan that will bring your goals to reality. To do this you will combine four variables into a unique and useful "Marketing Mix"—Product, Price, Place and Promotional Activities ("The 4 P's"). These four variables will define the path your product takes.

PRODUCT

As you plan a campaign you will make decisions about your specific product or service. If you have the ability, you can even determine how to package and deliver your product to your customer. Some things to consider include:

- product name (including the brand name)
- size and packaging
- product design
- product functionality
- warranty/replacement policy

PRICE

As mentioned in the case study "Flowers vs. Romance," I encourage you to focus on the benefits that your customers get from your product or service. Emphasizing benefits (rather than features) will allow you to charge a premium price. Some other pricing considerations include:

- wholesale vs. retail pricing
- cash, volume and early payment discounts
- bundling
- seasonal pricing
- market entry strategy

PLACE

This is also known as "channels of distribution." Where and how will your customers purchase your products or services? How will you ship them? Where are they stored until transport and how will you track inventory? Needless to say, each of these items will also contribute to the costs you incur and will need to be considered in your pricing strategy.

PROMOTIONAL STRATEGY

This element deals with the method(s) you use to communicate your product's value to your customers. It includes: promotional strategy, advertising, publicity and PR, and sales strategy. In this digital age you will also want to consider website and social media strategies for your products and services.

Putting the 4 P's into action requires you to design and implement a strategic marketing campaign. Here are the five steps necessary to designing a successful marketing campaign:

1. Set campaign objectives and determine the marketing mix (4 P's) for your campaign.
2. Design a strategy for promoting a product or services.
3. Create a step-by-step action plan that includes details, milestones, and "owners" for each detail.
4. Work your plan according to schedule to achieve critical milestones or benchmarks.
5. Evaluate and celebrate success!

Campaign Objectives

You know that you have a great product, a highly sought after service, and an engaging value proposition. But without a plan for promoting these things you will not have customers. Before you can design your campaign you need to set goals for expected outcomes and define the market segments you plan to target. This is done by clearly stating strategic campaign objectives.

Campaign objectives must be tied to your annual marketing goals. They should provide clear actions that will move towards accomplishing the larger goals you have set out in your marketing plan.

For instance, imagine that you manufacture custom-designed, high-end wood furniture intended to become family heirlooms. One of your annual marketing goals is to sell $150,000 worth of furniture to people living in a particular city. In Q1 of this year (January-March) you intend to conduct a marketing campaign targeting contractors and architects who deal in the luxury home market in your area. You want these professionals to help you generate a list of qualified leads and to make personal recommendations to homeowners.

Your objectives for this might be:
- Use direct mail and email marketing to build a list of 500 qualified homeowners in the area.
- Build relationships with 25 Architects, Realtors, and Home Builders who serve this market segment.

Campaign objectives need to have clear parameters of time and budget attached to them. A successful marketing campaign is a targeted initiative that catches the attention of a specific market segment in a set period of time. The clearer the focus in your campaign objectives, the more success you will have in your marketing campaign.

Your campaign objectives are:

_____

_____

_____

_____

_____

_____

_____

Campaign Strategy

Once you have your objectives clearly defined you can begin developing your campaign strategy. Figure 2.1 is a basic illustration of what a campaign strategy might look like while using the objectives discussed in the previous section.

The example shows the budget, timing and ownership of the activities for your Q1 campaign. From the table we can see that you intend to send a direct mail piece out in February. You are also planning to launch a Google Adwords™ drive in that same month. In March you have budgeted $100 for a "thank you" cocktail party. This party is a way for you to express gratitude to your key partners and new customers.

In addition, you are engaged in ongoing marketing activities such as blogging, an e-newsletter, and attending networking events. These items have their own budget line items. Note that while there are no financial obligations for blogging, your time is budgeted for in this chart. When you have completed your strategy, your campaign parameters and objectives will be clear and tied to your overall annual marketing goals.

Figure 2.1 - Q1 Campaign Strategy Example

Promotional Activity	Owner	Jan	Feb	Mar
Direct Mail Campaign	Me		$250	
Print Ads (or Google Adwords™)	Her		$150	
Media Release (PRWeb.com)	Him	$80		$80
eNewsletter	You	$35	$35	$35
Blogging (2x/month)	Me	$/hr	$/hr	$/hr
Networking Events	Me	$50	$75	$75
Referral Partner Meetings	Her	$50	$100	$100
Thank You Events	Him			$100
Budget Totals		**$215**	**$610**	**$390**

Promotional Activity	Owner	Month1	Month 2	Month 3
Budget Totals				

Campaign Design

It's time to get creative! You know what your campaign objectives are and have determined what tools you will use to implement those objectives. Now it is time to think about the message in terms of words and images. Go back to your Unique Value Proposition with your specific campaign in mind. What images will speak directly to the needs of your target audience? What messages will grab their attention? Remember, in your marketing campaign you are simply trying to get their attention and "rent out space in their mind." You don't have to close the deal yet. You want them to notice you so when they have a need that your product or service can provide they will think of you and be compelled to buy.

If you're not a creative type person, this is where you may need to enlist the help of a professional designer or creative agency. There is a local designer that I work with who knows my business quite well. We've done a lot of work together, and I like his style.

I usually have a few ideas in mind before I call "my guy," then he and I have a brief conversation and he's off and running. Within a day or two he will present me with some concepts that we can talk about and revise. Then it's time for him to finalize it. Keep in mind that every campaign is an extension of your larger brand. You want to grab a potential client's attention, but you don't want to diminish the work you have done to get you to this point. Having a designer or creative group who knows the bigger picture of your brand is very helpful.

If you don't have a professional designer I recommend you find one ASAP. Start interviewing potential individuals or agencies to see how they "fit." It's important that they share your core values and understand the mission of your company.

In the meantime there are some effective low cost options. I have listed three places below where you can put work out for bid to freelancers. The draw back here is that they tend to be single-effort opportunities. You don't usually end up creating a relationship with the designer, so he or she doesn't get to know you as well as a dedicated designer might. That may lead to disconnected pieces of your brand identity. But, for the short term, these options may work just fine.

Here are some resources that may be helpful:
- Fiverr® (fiverr.com) – People post things they are willing to do for 5 bucks. They can be quirky and off-the-wall, such as: "I will sing Happy Birthday to anyone you want wearing a goofy hat for $5."
- Elance® (elance.com) – This site provides instant access to thousands of professionals in various trades. Each has been rated by previous customers so you know what to expect before you buy.
- 99 Designs™ (99designs.com) – 99 Designs bills itself as "The #1 marketplace for graphic design, including logo design, web design and other design contests, with over 100,000 satisfied customers!"

Your campaign will use the following resources:

_____

_____

_____

_____

_____

_____

_____

_____

Schedule and Milestones

Your marketing campaign is beginning to take shape. You have: a) selected campaign parameters from your annual marketing goals; b) set campaign objectives and determined your marketing mix; and c) gotten creative with the details. Now it's time to develop a step-by-step action plan to focus on the tactical details of your campaign. This action plan is your campaign schedule. The four basic questions at this point are:

- What will be done?
- When will it be done?
- Who will do it?
- How will results be measured?

WHAT WILL BE DONE?

Do you plan on sending emails? Direct mail pieces? Putting up a billboard? Your creative activities have helped you decide the message content and delivery method.

This step will help you develop an executable plan. It may be a calendar with steps to be executed or a GANT chart to help you keep track of the details. This step is about project management as much as it is about creativity.

WHEN WILL IT BE DONE?

Each detail of your campaign will have its own time requirements and schedule. Some things demand that certain steps be completed before the next can be implemented. For example, if you intend to send out a direct mail piece, you have to create the piece first. You will establish an order for writing the piece, printing the piece, selecting addresses to whom it will be sent and stamping the envelopes before you head to the post office. Your schedule will keep you on track for completing each detail at exactly the right time.

WHO WILL DO IT?

This question provides accountability for your marketing campaign. You must assign ownership to each detail of the campaign and follow through with implementation and oversight. This question helps you know who to go to with specific questions. It also lets everyone know who is responsible for completing each task.

HOW WILL RESULTS BE MEASURED?

Setting a gauge (metrics) for each step of your campaign will allow you to determine if your campaign has been effective. One of the biggest challenges to any marketing endeavor is the ability to attach efforts to results. Without metrics you will not have the ability to know what worked and what didn't. This step will help you measure the return on your investment (ROI) of time and financial resources.

When the campaign schedule is set and metrics are established it's time to get to work. Follow the plan you have set and be sure to measure the results so you can evaluate your success (or failure) after the campaign is complete.

Evaluate Lessons Learned

If you have identified your market clearly, set SMART goals and objectives and followed the steps of your campaign, you will soon begin to see qualified leads coming into your sales funnel. A solid campaign schedule attached to clear objectives will keep you on track towards the completion of your marketing campaign. Once the campaign is complete it's important to set aside a dedicated time to take stock of the effectiveness of your proceedings.

This step is where you will note your successes and/or failures. Have you hit your targets? If yes, why? If no, why not? Were your campaign objectives effective? Were they targeted in the right place? Did you reach the right people? What could have been done better? What could have been left out? These are all questions you will want to address in your evaluation.

This step is also where you celebrate the work you have done. If you have reached your objectives you can celebrate knowing you are on track towards accomplishing your annual marketing goals. If you have fallen short, celebrate what you have done and take note of lessons learned for implementation next quarter.

Conclusion

In order to grow your business you need customers. A strategic marketing plan will help you find the right ones. Your strategic marketing plan, brought to life by campaigns, will capture the attention of and plant a seed in the mind of the customer so they remember you when they need you.

This book is designed to help you understand basic marketing concepts, clarify your marketing goals, and set strategic objectives for successful marketing campaigns. When you put the five core elements of this book together with the five steps of a successful campaign, customers will remember you and flock to you!

Here's to your success!

The Best Little Marketing Plan Templates

Once you have completed the worksheets for each section, you can transfer the information to these templates and you'll be ready to implement the marketing plan for your business!

Market Description:

_____

_____

Size / Geographic Locations: _____

_____

Demographics: _____

_____

Psychographics: _____

_____

Behaviors: _____

_____

☐ SWOT Analysis Complete?
(page 17)

Unique Value Proposition:

Market Position:

Core Products/Services:

1. Product .... Price ....

2. Product .... Price ....

3. Product .... Price ....

Annual Marketing Goals:

1. ....

....

2. ....

....

3. ....

....

Q1 Objectives:

Q2 Objectives:

Q3 Objectives:

Q4 Objectives:

Name .... Website ....

Fiscal Year .... Annual Marketing Budget ....

Latest Revision .... By ....

Campaign Strategy Template

Campaign Window: .... Campaign Budget: ....

Marketing Mix:

Product: .... Price: ....

Place: ....

Promotional Strategy: ....

Campaign Objectives:

1. ....

   ....

   ....

2. ....

   ....

   ....

3. ....

   ....

   ....

Campaign Strategy/Design:
(What tools or methods will you use, and how?)

Campaign Schedule/Milestones:

Name .... Website ....

Fiscal Year .... Annual Marketing Budget ....

Latest Revision .... By ....

Do you know the one thing that makes your business uniquely special? Dr. Sean Harry believes finding and developing that One Thing is the key to developing a thriving business.

Sean has spent his entire career helping individuals and organizations discover what makes them special and how to hone their unique value proposition to connect with their perfect clients, build the perfect work team, or find the perfect career.

With more than 10 years experience in corporate sales and professional development, Sean is known internationally for his seminars and workshops on topics related to brand engagement and building trustworthy relationships in business. As an advisor and adjunct faculty member for the Small Business Development Center (SBDC) at Portland Community College, Sean counsels business owners and teaches classes on how to start and grow successful businesses.

When not helping small businesses grow you can find Sean traveling with his wife Janeice, or working on a miniature dollhouse with his granddaughter Grace.

To learn more about Sean's training and coaching workshops, or to get booking information for your next event, visit www.DrSeanHarry.com.

ABOUT CHAIRSEVEN

Chairseven is an educational content production and creative studio, building digital learning platforms for students and professionals.

We believe that great learning tools foster a desire for greater knowledge. With this simple philosophy, we are working with extraordinary innovators in education to define the modern classroom as a place where students are not just better equipped to learn, but inspired to learn.

Discover more about Chairseven at www.chairseven.com.

39092 08976335 5

Made in the USA
San Bernardino, CA
22 January 2015

18633054R00032